PLANT DEFENSES

PLANTS THAT MIMIC

LOUELLA BATH

PowerKiDS press.

New York

Published in 2017 by The Rosen Publishing Group, Inc.
29 East 21st Street, New York, NY 10010

First Edition

Editor: Sarah Machajewski
Book Design: Reann Nye

Photo Credits: Cover David Clapp/Photolibrary/Getty Images; p. 4 Skorpionik00/ Shutterstock.com; p. 5 Sigur/Shutterstock.com; p. 6 Hayati Kayhan/ Shutterstock.com; p. 7 Max Sudakov/Shutterstock.com; p. 8 HHelene/ Shutterstock.com; p. 9 The Naked Eye/Shutterstock.com; p. 10 Roman Pyshchyk/ Shutterstock.com; p. 11 Olga_Anourina/Shutterstock.com; p. 12 Andreas Zerndl/ Shutterstock.com; p. 13 hallam creations/Shutterstock.com; p. 14 Hector Ruiz Villar/ Shutterstock.com; p. 15 Bildagentur Zoonar GmbH/Shutterstock.com; p. 16 Dennis van de Water/Shutterstock.com; p. 17 https://commons. wikimedia.org/wiki/File:Boquila_trifoliata.jpg; p. 18 Ed Reschke/Photolibrary/ Getty Images; p. 19 M Andy/Shutterstock.com; p. 20 Denise Kappa/ Shutterstock.com; p. 21 MCT/Tribune News Service/Getty Images; p. 22 Andrei Medvedev/Shutterstock.com.

Cataloging-in-Publication Data

Names: Bath, Louella.
Title: Plants that mimic / Louella Bath.
Description: New York : PowerKids Press, 2017. | Series: Plant defenses | Includes index.
Identifiers: ISBN 9781499421514 (pbk.) | ISBN 9781499421538 (library bound) | ISBN 9781499421521 (6 pack)
Subjects: LCSH: Mimicry (Biology)–Juvenile literature.
Classification: LCC B37 2017 | DDC 583'.04'18–d23

Manufactured in the United States of America

CPSIA Compliance Information: Batch #BS16PK: For Further Information contact Rosen Publishing, New York, New York at 1-800-237-9932

CONTENTS

MORE THAN MEETS
THE EYE 4

CHANGE AND SURVIVE . . . 6

ALL ABOUT
PLANT DEFENSES 8

MIMICRY
VS. CAMOUFLAGE 10

IS IT A BEE? 12

FIND THE FLY 14

A MASTER
OF DISGUISE 16

SKUNK CABBAGE 18

CORPSE FLOWER 20

THE NATURAL WORLD
OF MIMICRY 22

GLOSSARY 23

INDEX 24

WEBSITES 24

MORE THAN MEETS THE EYE

In the natural world, things may not always be what they seem. This is especially true when it comes to plants. Some plants fool us into thinking they're something they're not! They pull it off through mimicry. Mimicry is when a plant closely **resembles** something else, such as another plant or even an animal.

Mimicry is a special trait because not all plants have it. Plants that do have it use it in many ways. For some plants, mimicry helps them hide and stay safe from predators. Other plants use it because it helps them survive and make new plants.

Plants aren't the only living things that use mimicry. Can you find the butterfly in this picture?

CHANGE AND SURVIVE

Plants live in every kind of **habitat**, and each habitat has challenges for the **organisms** living there. These challenges could be a lack of sunlight, cold weather, or nasty predators. Over thousands of years, plants have developed ways of dealing with them.

Mimicry is a kind of adaptation. An adaptation is a change that helps a plant survive in its **environment**. Thousands of years ago, plants that displayed mimicry survived longer than plants that didn't. These plants passed on their traits to new plants, and the traits became part of the **species**. Today, some plants show that this adaptation is the key to their survival.

PLANT POINTER
Venus flytraps have a cool adaptation—they eat bugs!

Sundews appear to be covered in tiny drops of water. The "water" is actually a sticky substance that traps bugs looking for a drink! This trick helps the sundew catch the food it needs to be healthy.

ALL ABOUT PLANT DEFENSES

Adaptations help plants in many ways, especially when they're used as defenses. A defense is a way an organism **protects** itself. This is very important for plants because they can't run away from danger. There's a lot of danger in their habitats, including animals and bugs that want to eat them.

Some plants have stems that are covered with sharp **prickles**. Predators don't want to get too close to those plants! Smelling bad and looking sick are other plant defenses that keep predators away. One kind of plant closes its leaves when it's touched. In doing so, it survives another day.

PLANT POINTER
Mimicry is an uncommon defense! Few plants display this interesting trait.

This prickly stem sends a message: "Stay away!"

MIMICRY VS. CAMOUFLAGE

Mimicry is a cool plant defense. It works by tricking a predator into thinking the plant is something it's not. Predators might not eat or harm a plant if they think it's something else.

Mimicry is often grouped with camouflage, another kind of defense. Camouflage is when a plant blends in with its environment. Mimicry and camouflage are similar because in both cases the plants appear to be something they're not. The difference is that camouflaged plants don't want to be seen at all. They're great at hiding. Plants that mimic are seen, but as something different from what they really are.

PLANT POINTER
Herbivores are organisms that eat only plants. Deer and rabbits are common herbivores. Plants need to protect themselves from these creatures.

Living stone plants camouflage themselves to look like stones found in their environment. Cool!

IS IT A BEE?

Where's a good place to find bees? Flowers! Bees visit flowers in search of nectar. At the same time, they're also helping with **pollination**. Usually, a flower's bright color and sweet smell is enough to **attract** bees. The bee orchid takes it to another level by actually *looking* like a bee!

The plants look like a bee has landed on each pink flower. Actually, the "bee" is a part of the flower with brown and yellow markings. Male bees are drawn to it, thinking it's a female bee they can **mate** with. It isn't, but the bees pick up pollen and carry it to the next flower.

PLANT POINTER
Bee orchids also smell like female bees.

Bee orchids are masters of mimicry. They use it to make sure they're pollinated, which helps their species survive.

FIND THE FLY

Fly orchids use mimicry to look like a fly. This plant's flower has reddish-brown markings and is shaped like a fly's body. It smells like a female fly, too. The flower is surrounded by green leaves that wilt as it blooms. This makes the "fly" stand out even more to bugs looking for a mate.

The bugs are fooled and leave without a partner, but they do carry pollen with them. It's said that only a small number of fly orchids are pollinated this way, but the mimicry definitely helps—pollinated fly orchids produce more than 10,000 seeds!

Is this a flower or a bug? It's not always easy to tell.

15

A MASTER OF DISGUISE

One of the trickiest plants lives in the rain forests of Chile and Argentina. It's a vine that climbs up trees for support. What's amazing is that it doesn't just mimic one plant—it mimics many.

The *Boquila trifoliolata* changes the shape, size, color, and thickness of its leaves to match the plant it's growing on. For example, if the support plant has long, thin leaves, the vine will have long, thin leaves. If the same vine crosses over to a completely different tree, its leaves change to mimic the new tree. Scientists think the mimicry is a defense against plant-eating predators.

GIRAFFE WEEVIL

PLANT POINTER
The *Boquila trifoliolata* vine actually has two defenses: mimicry and climbing. Climbing keeps it off the ground, away from predators like weevils and leaf beetles.

The *Boquila trifoliolata* only shows its
natural leaves when it's growing on its own.

SKUNK CABBAGE

Flowers are known for smelling sweet, but not all of them do. In fact, some flowers mimic the smell of rotting flesh! The skunk cabbage is one of these fascinating plants.

The skunk cabbage is a wild flower that grows in forests and wetlands. The awful smell attracts bugs such as flies and beetles that feed on **decaying** matter. When the bugs visit the flower, they don't find food, but they unknowingly pick up the flower's pollen. When the bugs move on, they become **pollinators**. The skunk cabbage species survives, thanks to its clever—and smelly—mimicry.

The skunk cabbage is one of the only plants that can produce heat. It melts the snow around it!

CORPSE FLOWER

The corpse flower is a huge plant that sometimes smells like rotting flesh. The terrible smell mimics decaying matter to attract pollinators. However, the plant also displays another form of mimicry—its petiole looks like a tree.

A petiole is the part of the plant that joins the stem and the leaf. The corpse flower's leaf is huge, and the petiole could break easily if an animal ran into it. The plant protects itself by mimicking the colors and patterns of a tree trunk. Even though the plant isn't hard like a tree trunk, animals think it is. They avoid running into it.

PETIOLE

The bloom of a corpse flower is a big event. People come from all over to watch it! The flower smells really bad while it's blooming.

THE NATURAL WORLD OF MIMICRY

Plant mimicry is a very cool adaptation. However, it's pretty rare. That means that few plants have this awesome trait. The plants that mimic use it to attract the pollinators that can help their species survive. Plants also use mimicry as a defense against predators. Mimicry will likely help these plant species survive into the future.

Mimicry isn't just a defense found in plants. Many animals use it as a defense, too. In fact, sometimes they mimic plants in order to survive. The next time you see a green leaf or brown twig, look closer. Is it really what it seems?

GLOSSARY

attract: To draw nearer.

decaying: Rotting.

environment: The natural surroundings of a person, plant, or animal.

habitat: The natural home of an animal or plant.

mate: To come together to make babies. Also, each of a pair of animals or bugs that come together to make babies.

organism: An individual plant or animal.

pollination: The process of carrying pollen from one flower to another in order to produce seeds.

pollinator: Something that carries pollen between flowers.

prickle: A sharp growth on a plant stem.

protect: To keep safe.

resemble: To look or seem like something else.

species: A group of living organisms that have similar traits.

INDEX

A
adaptations, 6, 8, 22
Argentina, 16

B
bee orchids, 12, 13
bees, 12
beetles, 16, 18
Boquila trifoliolata, 16, 17
bugs, 6, 7, 8, 14, 15, 18

C
camouflage, 10, 11
Chile, 16
corpse flower, 20, 21

F
flowers, 12, 14, 15, 18,
         20, 21
fly orchids, 14

H
habitats, 6, 8
herbivores, 10

L
leaves, 8, 14, 16, 17, 20, 22
living stone plants, 11

P
petiole, 20, 21
pollen, 12, 14
pollinators, 18
predators, 4,
         16, 22

S
seeds, 14
skunk cabbag
species, 6, 13
sundews, 7

V
Venus flytraps
vine, 16

W
weevils, 16

WEBSITES

e to the changing nature of Internet links, PowerKic
eloped an online list of websites related to the sub
ok. This site is updated regularly. Please use this link
   list: www.powerkidslinks.com/plantd/mimc